745.5   Haas, Rudi.
Haa   Egg-carton zoo II

DATE DUE		PERMA-BOUND	
NOV. 6			

EGG-CARTON ZOO II

RUDI HAAS · HANS BLOHM · HEIKE BLOHM

EGG-CARTON ZOO II

RUDI HAAS · HANS BLOHM · HEIKE BLOHM

Toronto Oxford New York

OXFORD UNIVERSITY PRESS

Designed by Heike Blohm

Oxford University Press, 70 Wynford Drive, Don Mills, Ontario, M3C 1J9

Toronto Oxford New York Delhi Bombay Calcutta Madras Karachi
Petaling Jaya Singapore Hong Kong Tokyo Nairobi Dar es Salaam
Cape Town Melbourne Auckland

and associated companies in
Berlin Ibadan

Canadian Cataloguing in Publication Data

Blohm, Hans

Egg-carton zoo II

ISBN 0-19-540718-0

I. Haas, Rudi   II. Blohm, Heike, 1960-
III. Title.

TT870.B46 1989   j745.592   C89-090076-0

2 3 4 - 2 1 0 9

Printed in Hong Kong

TABLE OF CONTENTS

INTRODUCTION

The next time you open the refrigerator door, take a good look at that carton of eggs sitting quietly on the shelf. Do you realize that the seemingly humble egg carton in front of you is, in fact, an entire zoo full of animals? Don't just throw it in the garbage. Take your time and you will see that creatures of every size and shape imaginable are waiting to be released — by you. They are hiding behind each lump, bump and curve, and your imagination is the key that will set them free.

This book is your ticket to an amazing safari around the world. You will create and visit with animals that walk, fly, swim, crawl or bounce their way through life. You don't even have to be limited to this planet. Travel to lands beyond time where monsters munch, dinosaurs duel and dragons still remember how to breathe fire.

Rudi Haas is your tour guide. Listen and watch as he shows you discovery after discovery. But remember, he's been finding animals in egg cartons for a while now, so he's had lots of practice. Be patient and don't worry if you make a few mistakes. The material isn't costly and there's always another animal waiting around the next bend.

No need to pack. Just arm yourself with a small pair of scissors, a medium-sized egg carton and a large longing for adventure.

Beginning and Ending

You will need a pen or a fine-point marker for drawing your shapes. Small curved nail scissors work best for cutting out your zoo. A nail file can be used to smooth rough edges and to add texture to your animals.

It's best to practise with some simple shapes first and then move on to more complicated ones. Try looking at the carton from odd angles to see where the next animal is hiding. It may be staring right at you, but then again, it may be as well hidden as many animals are in nature.

By wrinkling, stamping or engraving, you can give the surface of your figures a variety of textures. No doubt you will invent some methods of your own. Shapes can be changed by softening the material with repeated finger pressure. And by holding a cut figure with tongs in hot water, it is possible to reshape the material while it is soft. **Do not use boiling water.**

Many household substances can be used to dye
your figures. Try experimenting with spices,
food colour, soya sauce, felt pens and shoe
polish. A few drops of hot water on instant
coffee powder or a pinch of saffron can do
wonders. Saffron, for instance, will give your
figures a permanent, deep, gold metallic glow.
You should add a few drops of dish detergent
to all water soluble dyes. This will help the
colour stick to the waxy surface of the carton.

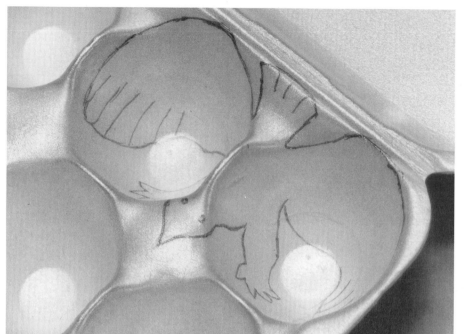

Eagles

Have you ever seen majestic eagles soaring and gliding in the sky? If you have, you know how they love to ride the wind as they hunt for dinner. Rabbits, reptiles, squirrels and fish are wise to take cover when they see an eagle's menacing shadow. With strong taloned feet, a sharp hooked beak, magnificent wings and incredible eyesight, the eagle is one of the animal kingdom's master hunters.

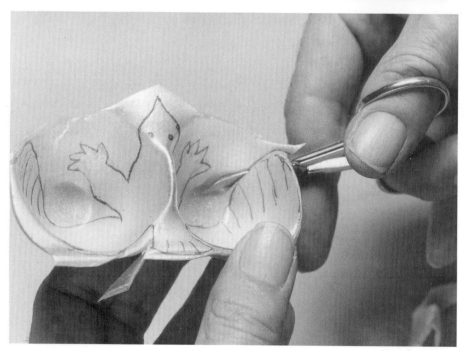

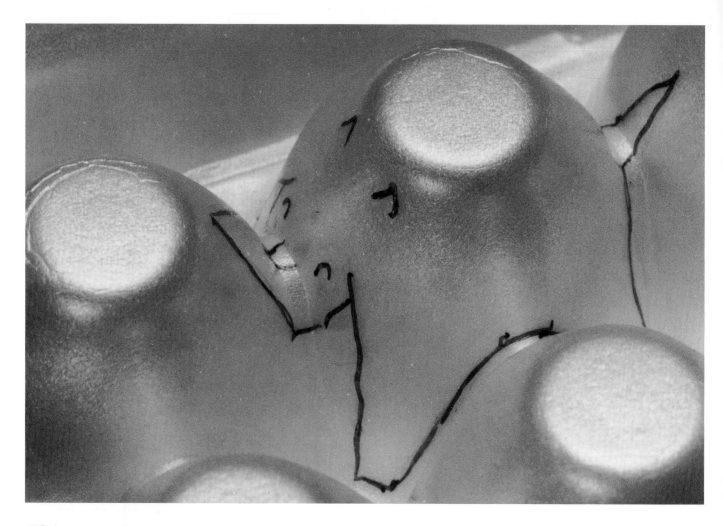

Rhinoceroses

The tank-like rhinoceros is a heavy, short-legged fellow with a massive body, thick skin and huge head. But don't let his looks fool you. He can run at amazing speeds when he's angry. This mammal, second in size only to the elephant, has a bad temper, sharp ears and a keen sense of smell. His horned nose makes a very effective weapon. But even nasty giants have their weaknesses. Rhinoceroses have poor eyesight and very little intelligence.

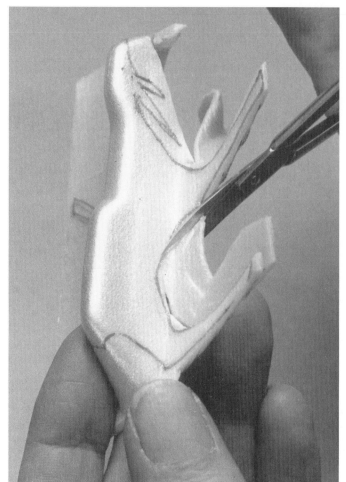

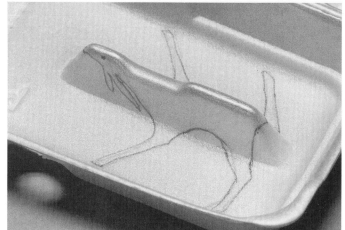

Gazelles

Gazelles like hot, dry plains and are found in southern Asia and Africa. The males usually have a pair of long, ringed horns which add to their beauty. Gazelles are dainty and very fast. They travel together in groups for protection, and often when they stampede, other animals are forced to run with them. Those who hesitate are in danger of being trampled. Sheep, goats and even lions have been seen running with a stampeding herd.

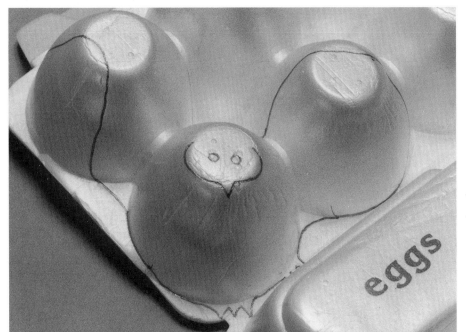

Owls

Whoooo hasn't heard of the wise old owl? Perhaps the huge wide-set eyes are what give him his knowing look. Owls are found in almost every type of habitat from the polar tundra to the tropical rain forest. They vary in size from the largest eagle owl to the smallest pygmy owl. These night hunters are able to fly silently, making it all the more dangerous for rodents, insects and smaller birds to be out after dark.

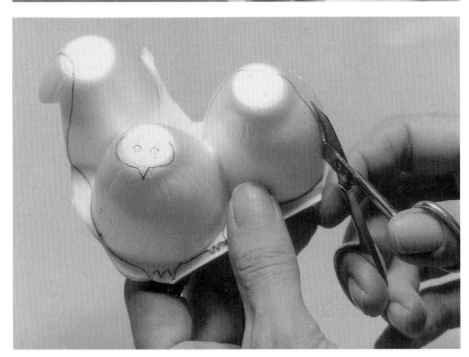

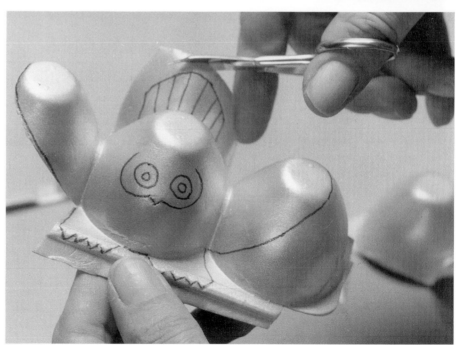

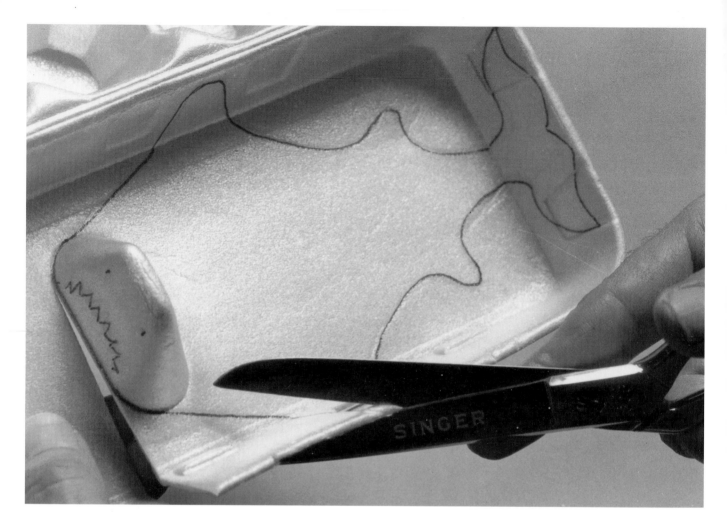

Sharks

Of the 300 known species of sharks, the whale shark is the largest. But it is probably the great white shark that most people think of and fear the most when they hear the word. Anyone who has seen the movie *Jaws* probably has not felt quite the same about swimming in the ocean since. These large creatures usually live in warm seas and feed mostly on other fish and marine animals. The shark rarely has dental problems. If he loses a tooth or wears one down, he simply grows another to replace it.

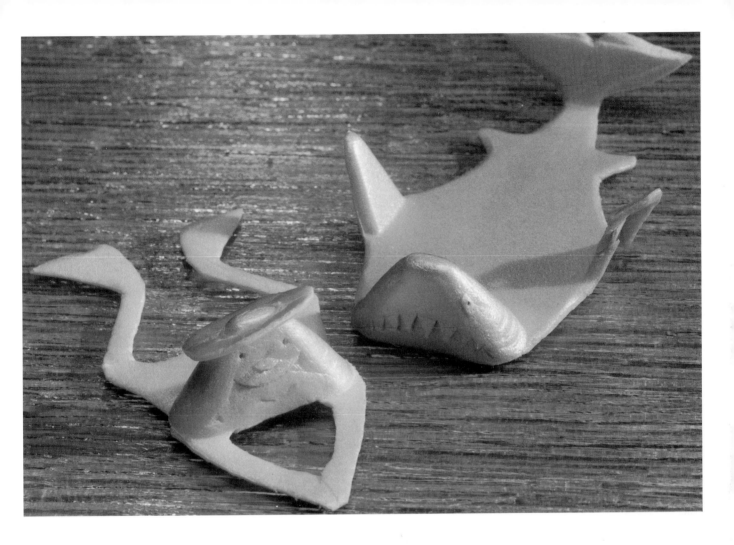

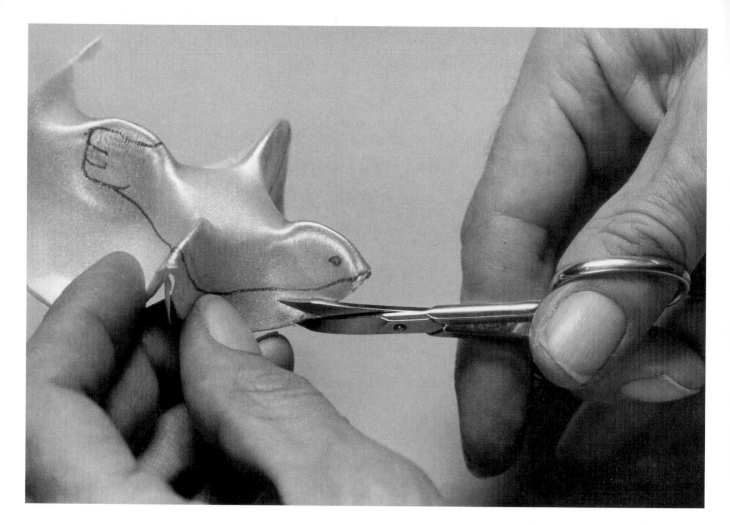

Seals

Awkward on land, but beautifully streamlined in the water, seals are marine animals with lots of personality. They are appealing crowd pleasers at zoos and aquariums and are easily trained to do clownish tricks. In the wild they live in large groups and feed on fish, molluscs and sea birds. Baby seals, or pups, are born on land and must be taught to swim by their parents.

Beavers

Beavers are sociable rodents who like to live in family groups. They are loyal and are believed to mate for life. Perhaps they are not the noblest looking of all the animals, but they are hard working and intelligent. They also happen to be fine engineers and dam builders. These qualities — plus the fact that beavers were highly valued for their fur — are why this animal was chosen as one of Canada's emblems.

Ducks

Just about everyone is familiar with ducks. Perhaps that is because there are more than 110 species throughout the world. One thing they all share is a love of water. Their webbed feet, water-repellent feathers and flat bills are perfectly suited for swimming, bobbing and dunking for food. If you ever hear a forecast for "ducky weather" run for your rain coat and rubber boots, but don't bother to quack. Quacking people aren't nearly as elegant as quacking ducks.

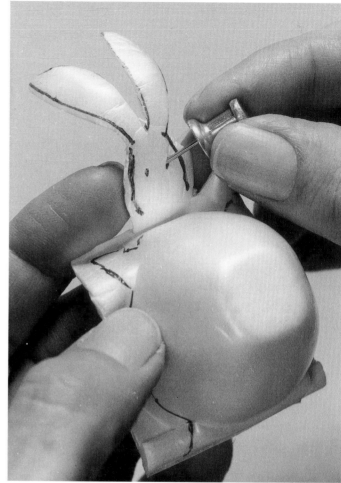

Rabbits and Hares

Bugs Bunny, Thumper, Peter Cottontail, the Easter Bunny...let's face it, most of us have lost our hearts to one rabbit or another somewhere along the way. But that furry, quiet creature you've always loved may, in fact, be a hare. It's very difficult to tell the difference, but generally hares are larger, faster and have longer hind legs and ears than rabbits. Young rabbits are born hairless and blind while hares are born fully furred and are able to run soon after they're born. Bugs! Have you been fooling us all this time?

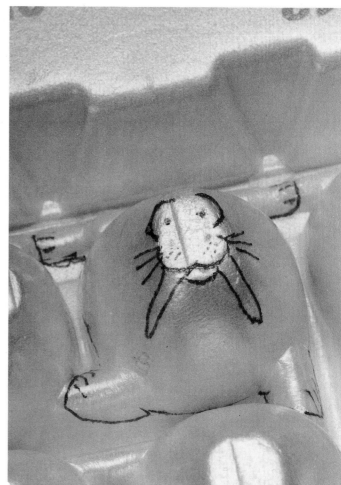

Walruses

If you've ever seen a walrus you'll know why its scientific name means "tooth-walking sea horse". Walruses often use their long tusks as levers to pull themselves out of the water and onto ice floes. Tusks are also useful when one walrus decides that his neighbour is taking up too much room. A friendly poke very effectively says, "Move over, you're hogging all the space."

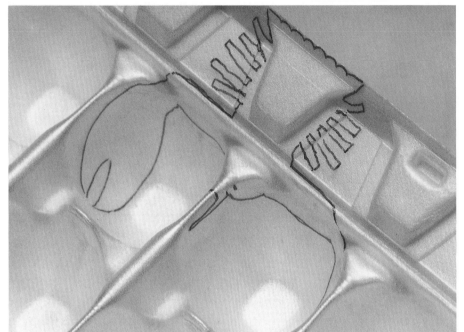

Water Creatures

Travelling to the underwater kingdom is like visiting another world. We so rarely get a chance to do it that most of us know very little about the creatures that live there. Some are drab and can easily blend with their surroundings, while others are flamboyant and very showy. Their shapes vary greatly too. Take the lobster, for instance. He is so fantastic that you probably couldn't dream up anything more unusual if you tried. But why don't you try anyway?

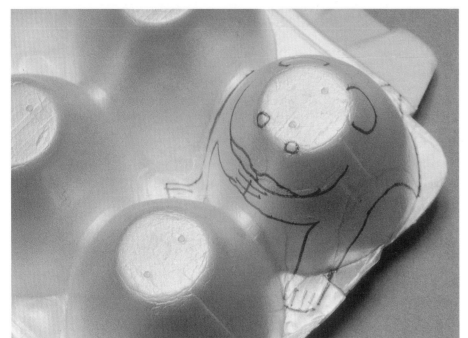

Koalas

Although they look like teddy bears and are often called bears, koalas belong to the marsupial family. Marsupials are animals that have pouches in which their young are carried and fed until they can fend for themselves. Koalas are found in Australia and were once hunted in great numbers for their fur. Today, they are protected in order to keep them safe from extinction.

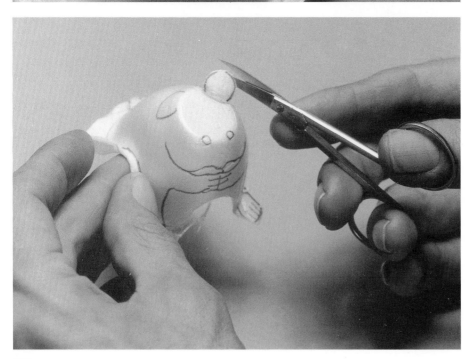

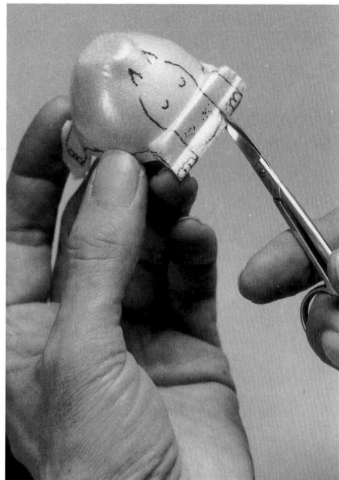

Hippos

Hippos are very large, barrel-shaped animals with short legs and huge heads. In spite of their heavy appearance, hippos can run well and are quite agile. But hippopotamuses are most at home in the water where they can float, sink and even walk submerged along the bottom for five to six minutes at a time. A baby hippo, or calf, nurses under water, can swim before it can walk and loves to hitch rides on its mother's back when she goes for a swim.

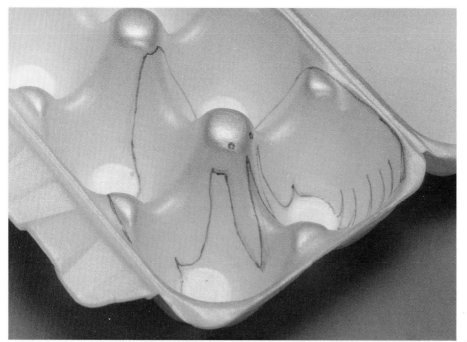

Pelicans

Pelicans are well known water birds with long beaks and amazing throat pouches. Most pelicans like to scoop their fishy lunches out of the water as they swim along the surface. But the brown pelican is a show-off. He prefers to fly along until he spots a fish from the air. Then he performs an amazing nose dive, plunges head first into the water and, if he's lucky, surfaces with his meal safely tucked in his pouch. Of course, sometimes all he gets for his trouble is a mouthful of water.

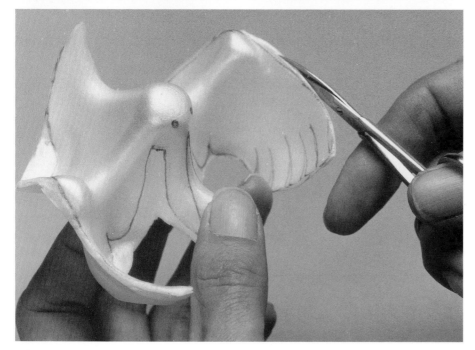

43

Frogs

The next time you are close to a river, pond, lake or swamp, you may have an opportunity to listen to one of nature's loveliest symphonies. A frog concert is a wonderful thing on a warm summer's night. Listen for the bass tones of the big bullfrog as he adds his voice to the higher trills of his smaller cousins. Frogs come in an amazing array of shapes, colours and sizes and have always been fascinating to watch as they develop from eggs to tadpoles to full-fledged members of the orchestra.

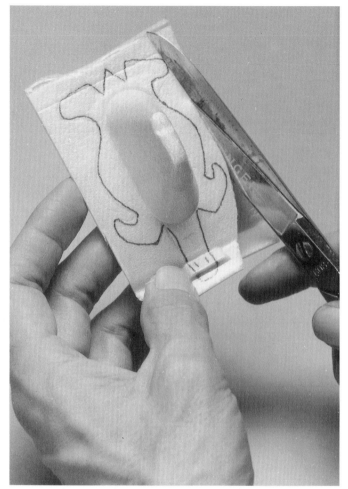
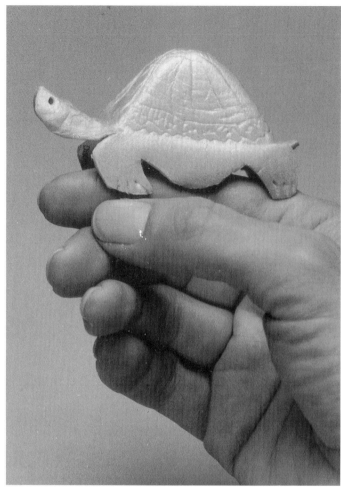

Turtles

Turtles have been roaming the earth and its waterways since the time of the dinosaurs. In fact, some turtle fossils have been found that date back more than 200 million years! Perhaps turtles owe their survival in part to the bony plates or shells that protect their bodies. Or maybe it's just that early on they learned to take life at a slower pace than the rest of us. Because of their simple basic shape, you should be able to find lots of turtles hidden in your egg carton.

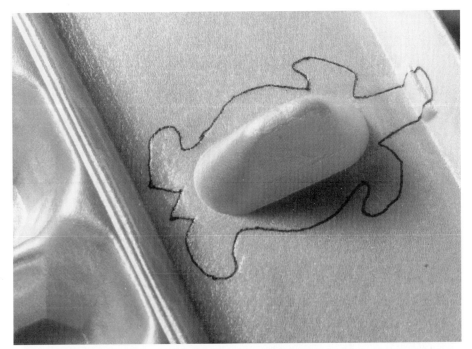

Going Wild

There was once a time when people believed that the earth was flat, and that if you sailed too close to the edge you would fall off. Many of the maps that were used back then carried the warning, "Here there be dragons." That warning no longer applies to the boundaries of our world, but maybe it should be added to the lids of all egg cartons. Here is your chance to let your imagination run wild. Here indeed there be dragons and dinosaurs and monsters and...?

Things To Do With An Egg-Carton Zoo

Just as there is no end to the creatures you can discover in egg cartons, there is no end to the fun you can have with them later. Make up stories and plays, make them into one-of-a-kind gifts, then wrap them in paper you print. Stick puppets, pendants, shadow boxes, game pieces — the list goes on and on. Collect bits of grass, wood, bark, mirror and stones and put your animals in their natural surroundings by making dioramas or scenes in a shoe box. Here we show a few ideas to help you get started. The rest is up to you!

Brooch

Animals with flat surfaces work best as brooches because they have enough room to glue the pin in place. Put a few drops of glue on the back of the animal and wait a few minutes. Gently place the pin into the glue. Be sure to wait until the glue is thoroughly dry before you pick the brooch up. Remember, these animals will crush easily so don't wear your new pin under your coat!

Materials:

- brooch pin
  (available in craft stores)
- white glue
- liquid plastic coating
  (optional)

Print Making

It's fun to make original giftwrap and cards with egg-carton animal prints. Cut your shapes from the flat lid. Remember that it's easy to make indentations on styrofoam if you want to give your prints interesting textures. A fingernail is a perfect tool. Choose a paint or ink pad and coat one side of your animal. Place the animal paint side down on the paper and press firmly. If you prefer, you can place the paper on top of the coated shape and rub it down with a wooden spoon. This procedure can be repeated many times to give interesting patterns. It isn't necessary to paint the shape each time. Images made with less paint will be fainter and can give your finished product a nice effect. Different papers will give different results. As always, it's best to experiment a little.

Materials:

- paper
- paint or ink
  (fingerpaints, ink pads,
  acrylics, poster paints)
- wooden spoon
- small paint brushes

Christmas Tree Ornaments

It's always nice to look at your Christmas tree and see something you made hanging on it. Egg-carton birds and animals make perfect ornaments and, if handled carefully, will be a source of pride year after year.

Thread the needle with approximately 30 cm of thread. Loop the thread through a button and tie a good strong knot. Holding the animal in one hand, carefully poke the needle up through the centre of the animal's back. Pull the thread through the hole until the button is tucked snugly inside the animal. Remove the needle and tie the thread to make a loop at the top.

Materials:

- large buttons
- heavy thread
  or embroidery silk
- sewing needle

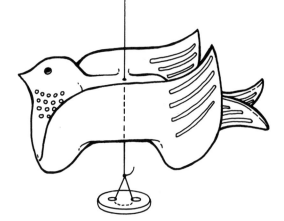

Mobile

Prepare your animals just as if you were making Christmas tree ornaments. Now cut the wire into three or four pieces of different length. The longest wire will be at the top and the shortest will be at the bottom. Make a loop at each end of all the pieces as shown. Tie an animal onto each loop.

It is best to start with simple mobiles and graduate to more complicated ones later. To assemble your mobile start with the piece that will hang at the bottom. Find the balancing point of the wire (with animals already attached), and wind a long piece of thread around it. Fasten it with a knot and dab a bit of white glue on the knot to hold it in place. Fasten the other end of the thread to the balancing point of the next wire up in the same manner.

Materials:

- large buttons
- heavy thread
- white glue
- thin wire
  (florist's wire works well)
- scissors

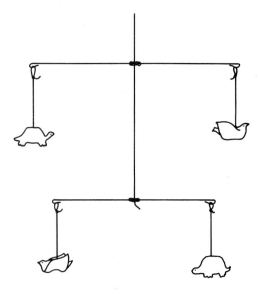

Checker Set

This one is easy, but you will need lots of patience. You will also need a checker or chess board. Be sure to choose animals that are small enough to sit nicely on one square. Twenty-four pieces are needed in all — twelve for you and twelve for your opponent. If you decide to make all your animals the same, be sure to dye twelve with one colour and twelve with another. If you decide to do two different types of animals in your set, make twelve of one kind and twelve of the other. Turtles make ideal checker pieces, but you may think of something even better.